This book is dedicated to all the little colorful eccentric dinosaurs!

ROAR !! LOUD!!

WRITTEN AND ILLUSTRATED BY
NICK HARBORNE

ROARY the Radical Raptor loves to play! Let's watch the colors of the RAINBOW guide his way!

RED is the color
of love and heat.
It's the color of apples,
so juicy and sweet!

ORANGE is the color
of autumn and fun!
It's the color of
pumpkins,
and the
setting sun!

YELLOW is the
color of **lemons**, so tart.
Like a sweet lemonade,
it will refresh
your heart!

GREEN is the color of all that's alive. With plants and creatures that thrive and survive!

BLUE is the
color of the **sky** up high!
With clouds that drift,
and birds that fly!

INDIGO is the
color that's deep and dark.
It's the color of night,
with stars that spark!

VIOLET is the color of elegance and grace.
It's the color of **butterflies**,
that flutter and chase!

ROARY

loves all the colors,
each and every one.
And now you know them too,
for lots of colorful fun!

The RAINBOW
is a wonder, full of delight.
And you are too,
with all your colors
so bright!

THANK YOU FOR JOINING ROARY ON THIS COLORFUL ADVENTURE!

The fun doesn't stop here! More books, stories, and
coloring books featuring Roary the Raptor are coming soon!
Stay tuned for exciting new friends, captivating worlds,
and unleash your creativity with our

ROARY COLORING BOOKS!

Follow us on social media for updates and sneak peeks!
Get ready for more magical moments!

@ROARYRAPTOR

Wishing you endless colorful adventures,

NICK HARBORNE

COLOR ME!

Manufactured by Amazon.ca
Acheson, AB

11304983R00017